GOD IS A LAUGHING BEDOUIN

Copyright © 2017 Cullene Bryant

Except for the use of short passages for review purposes, no part of this book may be reproduced, in part or in whole, or transmitted in any form or by any means, electronically or mechanically, including photocopying, recording, or any information or storage retrieval system, without prior permission in writing from the publisher.

The publisher gratefully acknowledges the support of the Canada Council for the Arts and the Ontario Arts Council for its publishing program. The publisher is also grateful for the financial assistance received from the Government of Canada through the Canada Book Fund..

Cover design: Val Fullard

Library and Archives Canada Cataloguing in Publication

Bryant, Cullene, author
    God is a laughing bedouin / Cullene Bryant.

(Inanna poetry and fiction series)
Poems.
Issued in print and electronic formats.
ISBN 978-1-77133-461-7 (softcover). -- ISBN 978-1-77133-462-4 (epub). --
ISBN 978-1-77133-463-1 (kindle). -- ISBN 978-1-77133-464-8 (pdf)

    I. Title. II. Series: Inanna poetry and fiction series

PS8553.R912G64 2017   C811'.54   C2017-902171-0
                                                                                                                                                                                C2017-902172-9

Printed and bound in Canada

Inanna Publications and Education Inc.
210 Founders College, York University
4700 Keele Street, Toronto, Ontario M3J 1P3 Canada
Telephone: (416) 736-5356 Fax (416) 736-5765
Email: inanna.publications@inanna.ca Website: www.inanna.ca

MIX
Paper from responsible sources
FSC® C004071

GOD IS A LAUGHING BEDOUIN

POETRY BY
Cullene Bryant

Inanna Poetry & Fiction Series

INANNA Publications and Education Inc.
Toronto, Canada

ALSO BY CULLENE BRYANT

Llamas In The Snow
In the Dry Woods

*As always, to my children, Alex and Rhiannon.
And to my wonderful grandchildren who bring such joy to my life:
Ava, Dalia, Luke, Teya, and Vivian.
You are all my greatest works, and my love is with you always*

Contents

CHILDHOOD

Calling of a Six year Old Child I	3
Calling of a Six Year Old Child II	4

YOUTH

Embarking I	9
Embarking II	11

VOCATION

Chaplain's Welcome	15
Intensive Care Unit	16
Geoffrey's Memorial Service	17
Chart No. 8275	18
Lung Cancer	19

MARRIAGE AND DIVORCE

Oval With Points: Henry Moore	23
Betrayal	24
Mary Magdalene	25
Phone Calls 1973	26

When She Visits	28
How I Walked On Water	30
Daughter's and Mother's Lament	31
Wedding Dance	32
The Garden	33

MOTHERHOOD

Swimmer	37
Drummer	38
Immaculate Conception	39
Pietà	41
Crucifixion	42
Resurrection	43

LOVE AFFAIRS

Dreams While Considering A Second Marriage	47
Never Travel To Montana You Could Get Snowed In	49
Passion	50
Rival	51
After the Affair	52

SECOND MARRIAGE

Rose	57

Meditation (Riffing on *Muse* by David Zieroth)   59
A Real Gentleman   60

WIDOW

Enchanted Evening   65
Woman of Samaria   67
Grandmother   68
Question   69

FINAL CURTAIN

Gethsemane   73
The Trial   75
At My Dying   78
Make My Coffin Wide   79
Last Act   81

AFTERWORD   83

CHILDHOOD

Calling of a Six-Year-Old Child I

Ocean spray beaded on my father's brow gone to England
to earn fellowship in the Royal Academy of Physicians and Surgeons

Salty tears sting my face sleepless in bed
I gaze at stars they hang over London too

A large white moon floats in the sky
spotlight beckons the actor on stage
my harbour light calling me home
the white of God's eye

Breezes blow all the way from Eli's temple
curtains flutter smell of camel dung cypress incense
sand in my wondering eyes
wind fans cheeks dries tears

Three times I hear a lyre a harp a bell
You called I lisp into the night
God whispers *See the stars in the sky*
sands on the seashore
unnumbered immeasurable my love for you

The covenant is made
as with Abraham and Sarah and all those who followed
you shall be mine and I shall be yours
Berith inscribed upon my heart

Calling of a Six-Year-Old Child II

Jesus healed ten lepers
sent them to the priest
to be examined
declared clean
only one returned
gave thanks
said to Jesus

We've met before
You were six years old
when Mary packed a lunch
and went to market
to buy fresh fish and pomegranates

You wandered down a lane
spied a beggar in the ditch
dug deep into your bag
full of food found a melon
cut and quartered

Just as you reached out to me
fruit dripping juice
Mary yanked your hand
away from mine
Never touch a leper Mary said

At midday you returned
Take this bread
fresh from the baker's oven

I grabbed the loaf
You fell hands and feet bloodied
cried ran back to Mary's embrace

Jesus nodded
I remember it was
when you broke the bread

YOUTH

Embarking I

All the way to Jerusalem I travelled
alone photographed David's mosque
rode an Arab's horse
to Petra city of red rocks
women scarved in black prayed
in the church of the Our Father
walked the road to the cross

All the way unseen, God followed
jingled coins in my blue jeans' pocket
while I bartered in the market place
for an Aramaic cross to wear
around my neck sat across
from me at a marble table
tasted goat's cheese sipped a glass
of Galilean wine in Bethlehem
just beyond the souvenir shops
a Bedouin appeared swathed
in white down to his sandals proffered
coffee camel rides Arabian sweets
pointed to blue window frames
everywhere *For good luck*
We have a saying here there's the blue of the sky
blue of the sea blue of a woman's eyes
He looked straight into my black pupils

But all your women's eyes are brown
Mine too He winked
offered me his arm but I hung back
not knowing all the while
God is a laughing Bedouin

Embarking II

When Jesus left home at thirty
Mary called the limo to get him to Jordan
on time when he went
forty days into the wilderness
she gave him a cell phone *Call
before midnight devil or no*

When he overturned the money changer's
table in the temple she chided
What would Uncle Benny say?
Control yourself

But when he went to Jerusalem she bowed
her head and wept   packed a bag lunch
bread and fish a nice bottle of Galilean
wine kissed him on the cheek
God go with you

When my son left for college I called
a taxi to take him to the airport
gave him a calling card *Phone me*
told him to mind his manners in church

If he had gone to Jerusalem
a war or some demonstration
placards tear gas rage
at right-wing government

photo in newspaper voice on public radio
I would have dragged
him home back to the carpentry shop
basement locked the door
paid Judas off got a fake passport
plane ticket to the Outer Hebrides
No one would have called me Holy Mother

VOCATION

Chaplain's Welcome

The vice-president of operations welcomed me to the hospital
state of the art world class cutting edge
assured me clients appreciated our product
promised a half time maybe one FTE in my department
although we're downsizing
gave me a whirlwind tour of the ICU
introduced head nurse of the transplant program
management functions at optimal efficiency
pointed out new electro monitoring system
neo-natal incubators graph machines in clinic
shook my hand *so glad you're part of the team.*

I went to my office sorted out
quality assurance reports explained
my role and function at nursing grand rounds
formulated goals and objectives at the end
of day organized a communion kit
in case a client wanted
a component of spiritual care
rode glass elevator to basement

congratulated myself for
joining the health care industry

Intensive Care Unit

over here Cree man pierced lung
knifed by his own wife last time she'll suffer black eye broken wrist
over there college student brain dead late
for work at McDonalds ran headlong into truck on Calgary Trail
parents in Quiet Room wait for another son flying
from Toronto before they turn respirator down
that teen-age girl renal failure moving soon to palliative unit
in this peculiar wasteland plastic snakes slither
between parched lips down throat
syringes scorpion tails attached to plastic
tubes sting flesh
green-eyed monitors stare at face of old man
hold court at foot of bed graph heart beats
in this sterile land
where is hope?
look above green curtains medicine cupboard metal chart containers
a cloud hovers by day pillar of fire by night

Geoffrey's Memorial Service

We crept softly on crepe soles filed into chapel
neat orderly line faces drawn
lifted Joanne read the part
about Jesus receiving the children
Liz gave personal remarks
Geoff's parents had flown back to Grande Prairie
held their own funeral
the chaplain talked about peace while
most of us cried and wondered
why we kept him alive on the respirator
sent him for multiple surgeries

He lived ten months in neo-natal
a few of us wished he'd drowned
in the amniotic fluid of his mother's womb
he never sucked her breast nor
did she hold him in her arms
no one knew for sure he would die
nor what kind of life he might have had still
we made some advances in medical science

His case has been recorded in two
international journals subject of a lecture
offered to medical students in the second term

They provided coffee and cookies after the service
but none of us could stay
we had to finish our shift

Chart No. 8275

Book him for surgery   *Tomorrow*
triple bypass   *Complex operation*
You know the routine   *Only God knows*
Try him on the new drug   *Pray for us sinners*
the Americans market   *Now and at the hour of our death*
experimented with pigs   *Doctors know what they're doing*
We think it works   *Don't take chances*
Could be a reaction   *Tomorrow*
Good candidate, though   *A fighter*
compliant and not overweight   *That's what I've always been*
He'll make it   *I'll make it*

How are you doing? I'm the
    social worker   *I'm scared*
Are you strong enough to fill out
    these forms?   *My strength is in Thy right hand*
I'm the dietician   *I'm scared*
You'll be on solids next week   *Man cannot live by bread alone*
I'm your new nurse   *I'm still in pain*
Have your bowels moved yet?   *The Lord giveth and the Lord taketh*
You'll be transferred to a general
    unit tomorrow   *Blessed be the name of the Lord*
Congratulations   *I survived*

Lung Cancer

I want to die Louie groaned
sat upright in bed arms thin as a bird's leg
reached for the horizontal bar straightened
his back sputtered gasped
He's going to die nurse whispered
*He's having anxiety attacks Can you stay
hold his hand?* she fixed the IV tubes
I won't leave you I said *Breathe deeply*
His hand a claw in mine whites of his eyes
I sat with him all morning
The doctor wrote in his chart
while Louie heaved and sighed
At last his wife came *The car broke
down I would have been here earlier*
She took my place his hand *This is a hard
time for you* I said
*God is good The mechanic
fixed the car right away when I told him
about my Louie We had a great life
together ten years he's my second husband so sweet
to me* She kissed and stroked his hand
The doctor finally came with morphine
Louie slept and breathed
The next day he and his wife played cards at the bedside table.
I still want to die he held the joker in his hand *I'm ready*
God is good said his wife *We have another day*
A week later Louie was labeled chronically depressed

Just let me die he said *I'm ready*
The nurse gave him Ativan a relaxant then
God was good it happened three weeks later.

MARRIAGE AND DIVORCE

Oval With Points: Henry Moore

you sit in the round sculpture
green patina worn to a burnished bronze
grasp two points at the centre
almost meet enough space for your fist
God's finger touching Adam's
or you reaching never quite meeting me
while time holds us a second
in its oval arms

ancient bronze statues do not survive stolen
melted down to make weapons of war
stone and ceramic endure
once in a Princeton garden
now this maquette languishes in
the University Art Museum

Betrayal

A morsel dipped into a bowl signified betrayer
We watched him walk away slam door
We thought since he carried
the money box in his coat pocket
he left to buy more food wine
much appreciated
Why didn't we notice the signs?
Later, someone said he pilfered money
didn't give to the poor bought drinks
for the high priest's soldiers

Call it denial lack of perception
or did we trust too much
one of the original twelve?
Who was to blame for the traitor's kiss?
Was it our fault for being so naïve?

Every time I think of
the look on Jesus' face
when he dipped the bread
passed it on to Judas
I could hang myself for not
picking up the clues
signs everywhere

Jesus didn't say a thing nor
point a finger
We were all singing when
he led us to the Mount of Olives

Mary Magdalene

Who knows the true story
why she came that night to say
goodbye before his death poured oil
of nard over his feet already wet
with kisses anointed
his body with tears
let down her hair wiped away grief
eyes shining love
Your faith has saved you Jesus said arms outstretched
in blessing on the night our marriage
ended I wasted tears
anointed him extravagantly
one last time nothing was saved
eyes like an owl at night accusing
hard piercing no sacrament of forgiveness
he left me with a memory of indifferent arms

Phone Calls 1973

Telephone lines stretched tight dip and climb
eastward back to where I left you
Our connection then in
hands held kisses
our own dandelion wine hearty dinner
served to friends
Now in static
we communicate
pauses phrases disconnections *How are the children?*

Last summer when I came to visit
to talk about sending
more money show you the college brochures
for our son it was old times
glass of wine seafood salad you paid
told the joke about my sister
found out about George and Maisie
You've done a good job with the kids.
Friendship warmer than married love
memories of *Do you love me?* Gone

Birds fly over telephone wires
seeking sun escaping cold
keeping spring alive
from place to place season to season
in song and feather down

They forget hunter's bullet
grazed wing
fallen one fly on
rest in new meadows greening trees

When She Visits

What you do
what you're supposed to do is
take our daughter on your knee
put your arm around her like so
I'll demonstrate show you how to give affection
Before she was born
you sat in your armchair
sipped scotch
smoked a pipe
peered over the newspaper rustling
head cocked to the side
glanced at us on the floor
instructed our son
Have a lady fight Be gentle.

I was pregnant
You should have got down on all fours
wrestled with our five-year-old boy
instead of scanning headlines
ceasefire in Vietnam   Watergate
manned skylab mission

Ice still tinkles in your glass
when she visits
sits on the rug looks up
waits for you to reach down
lift her into your lap and
bury your beard into her blushing cheek

If I lived with you now I would hurl the glass
into the fireplace burn the newspaper
overturn your chair and all

How I Walked on Water

after work cook a quick dinner
my children and I sit at the table by kitchen window
watch our dog play in snow
chat about the day's events
kids scrape plates feed dog watch TV
do homework I practice Stephen Sondheim
make a fire write a poem
a woman friend appears on doorstep sits on sofa knits winds up
tangled yarn into neat balls
more mulled wine
dishes sit in sink laundry unfolded
floor should be swept wait 'til Friday
divorce isn't so bad

Daughter's and Mother's Lament

I don't want to wear
your wedding veil
it's cursed from the divorce

What to do with wedding ring white prayer book I carried
down the aisle orchids
dried and crumbled long ago
I should put these tokens in a hope chest
for a granddaughter
sell them at a thrift shop
give the wedding dress to the Salvation Army

What to do with love that lingers
after phone calls meetings
her plane gets in at seven o'clock
the kids are at my place this Christmas
I'll send you pictures
see you at her graduation concert wedding

First love father of my children

Go to chapel light candles pray
for the new woman in his life
always bless him on his way

Wedding Dance

parents of the bride we move to the centre
our dance not a slow old-fashioned waltz
but the fifties jive that rock and roll rhythm
arms taut bodies apart a jerk of your hand pulls me close
I twist under your arm you fling me away
never missing a beat of that rock and roll rhythm

a few weeks ago Celeste on the phone long distance
to Vancouver *what tune will you dance to, Mom?*
laughing I say *your father and I loved
that rock and roll rhythm.*

grinning panting sweating
hips swing hands grasp let go when
he swung me away that last time
I tripped dizzy lost the throb
of that rock and roll rhythm our fingers
never connected again his arm never circled my waist
except for this dance at our daughter's wedding
never missing a beat of that rock and roll rhythm

The Garden

Eve frightened child garden pillaged
could have stamped her foot on the snake's head
'til yellow eyes bulged from sockets
marbles in the dirt Eve
angry girl could have ripped a branch
from the tree of life whittled a point stabbed the creature
right between his eyes a bloody head her trophy

Eve jealous maid could have
stoned the snake 'til the tongue lolling
between sharp teeth lay grit covered discarded
ribbon in the dust instead

Eve with bare hands grasped twisting serpent
wound the convoluted body round her torso
tightly round her waist green and shimmering
let it slide between her breasts the head nestle
just at the nape clothed in this girdle womanly
she sallied out of the garden into the world.

MOTHERHOOD

Swimmer

I watch her rise my daughter
wet strands of seaweed hair translucent
shoulders gleaming learning siren's song

Bubbles surface fringe her arms and legs
Aphrodite sprung from sea foam
dripping pearls

I reach out to pluck water lily bud
catch sea nymph toss her laughing
into salty air and frothy brine

But she quick fish
slips my clumsy grasp the one
who swam leisurely in my belly's
waves no more my water baby

Drummer

Drum sticks fly in angry air thick
with broken promises
cymbal's clash rends
soundless night shrieks rage
against pollution war technology
endless injustices of an evil age like
French grip ghost notes polyrhythm
Atlas juggles golden apples
holds up the sky

Why did I rejoice when you kicking
leapt out of my loins into the black vacuum
of a lost world too soon your
soft kissed cheeks bearded black
too soon your milk sweet gurgle
voiced a desperate shout
uncurling fingers grasped sticks
rhythm driven struck empty into air

Immaculate Conception

I wonder how it happened when the Holy Spirit
came upon her a soldier
on the corner side street in Nazareth
sweating in his uniform too big for
him belonged to his uncle who died
in the last war spots a young Jewess
carrying a jug of water on her head
He steps up demands a drink pours
all of it over his face licks
his lips salty
I want more than a drink, girl

Squinting in the sun she cannot
see his smirk fingers claw
just above her elbow sleeve torn
vessel smashed she is overshadowed

A great white dove
soars down from heaven blinded
by the sun she cannot
see what knocks her down
her head hits the rocks skin
of upper thigh scratched raw
smothered by wings mouth stuffed
with feathers she is overshadowed

An ecstatic vision as when Moses hidden
in a cleft of rock saw God's back
glide by in clouds

or as when Jacob wrestled
with the angel and limped
away at dawn this time
when God passed by he let her see his thigh
his mortal penis he wounded
in the groin fell
softly on the grass
he was overshadowed

When the Holy Spirit came
upon her Mary wept
washed blood from her legs
hid behind locked doors
afraid to tell her mother
ashamed kept silent
until the inevitable

Pietá

Yesterday Mary rocked Jephtha's daughter
in her arms Tamar and the Levite's concubine

Today she cradles Korean comfort women
Nigerian girl kidnapped trafficked sold
a Filipina pokpok under
an Australian salesman
on his sex tour Syrian girl raped in Za'atari
married to restore her family's honour a Nepalese child bride
given to a merchant twice her age in Guinea a girl is cut her
genitalia made pure pleasing her sexuality controlled
Mother Mary arms
heavy with women's pain
embraces mends heals broken-hearted
broken-spirited bruised
and bleeding Corpus Christi

Crucifixion

Who held Mary
when they took Jesus
from the cross

No arms strong enough
no voice soft enough
no cloth cool enough
no song sweet enough
to bear the burden   sorrow
nothing stopped her tears

And where was God
the father
when Jesus hung his head and died

No storm loud enough
no sky dark enough
no waves high enough
no quake big enough
to bear the burden   sorrow
nothing stopped God's tears

Resurrection

John took Mary home
cup of warm soup
fresh linen on the bed cozy quilt

But she couldn't sleep
what mother could
after the day's events
She rose tip-toed
into a field of daisies
stood knee deep in wild flowers
shivered rubbed tired eyes
to greet the dawn there he stood
Jesus she cried ran embraced

He let her touch muscled arm broad chest
rough cheek softly textured robe

Mother he said *Don't go to the tomb*
with the other women rest a while
She laid her head on his shoulder
He stroked her hair not a sound
not larks mourning doves nor angel choirs broke
the sacred silence while he held
rocked his mother in his arms

LOVE AFFAIRS

Dreams While Considering a Second Marriage

1.

Caught i stand still immobile
in a warehouse storage room beside furniture
lined row on row

Reflected in their polished surfaces
flames mirrored orange yellow fire in my eyes

Unseen arsonist lurks
behind closed door smoking wood walls

2.

My lover lies beside me on the bed
window at his right open
to green fields swaying grass

We do not touch caress
each other hopeless paralyzed
I await his death

He flies to open the door

Drifting softly floating cushioned
on grass sprinting into wind vanishing

I lie still listen to breeze blowing over

tulips bulbs burst push up soil
leaves splayed to sun

I fly to open door
I run into spring run for my life

3.

he tries to teach me to drive better
buys a new frying pan mine is scratched
shows me how to scramble an egg without burning the underside
tells me to iron his drip dry shirts
wants me to learn to ski improve my golf swing
use his mother's detergent whiter wash
I just want to be proud of you
make it better help

i dream large green scales
hair-tangled i try to uproot pull out
at beauty salon show hairdresser green sprouts
help woman soft-handed
pours oil on my head
delicate fingers massage skull kneads mind
anoints me singing
i am

Never Travel to Montana You Could Get Snowed In

In snowy Montana (derivative Spanish)
you said marry me
marriage (mar'ij) state of being married
a close union merry me said
no this state is not to be travelled in
too many shining mountains
claustrophobia (L claustria) fear of enclosed spaces

mer-ry (mer'e) adj. full of fun festive
merrymaker n. me (me) pron. objective case

In Montana I said no
to merry you I remain
an unmarried merry subject

Passion

Fall in love with Jesus she says
Easy for her Irish nun trained and cloistered
contours of her body hidden behind habit
white linen wimple covers hair neck cheeks
Jesus is my lover written
on poster tacked to her bedroom door
Shall I love Jesus only
as I grow old my breasts sag skin slack
pubic hair no longer black and tangled
but a Van Dyke beard silken grey

Then I'll call Him in the hush of night
think only of prayers

Rival

i love you less than before
you write her name behind closed door
facebook skype and e-mail letters
leaves my heart quite untethered
i'll break the clasp of your golden chain
leave your toolbox in the rain
rip the sheets from off our bed
tear your underwear to shreds
when all of this is done and more
i'll slip behind that closed door
shout my name on twitter
create a profile on Tinder
get the app for instagram
and prove to all your love's a sham

After the Affair

Snap flick switch
my gas fire burns
Polished hardwood floor
reflects orange flare

Across worn Persian rug
small balcony glass door
beyond city's bright lights I sit
Moses at burning bush
no incredible heat
warms my bare feet
no voice intrudes

My restless eyes look
across living room through
darkening glass
automobile headlights
jostle apartment
windows flicker
neon signs wink

Filigree bridge bears traffic to city
stretches slender limbs over black water
flashing yellow orange   green

a fire burns there
I long to plunge
into its depths
swim to shore
crawl up rocks and greet people on Main Street
but they have all gone home
and stand behind locked doors

By my still fireplace I sit musing
immobile like the bridge gazing.

SECOND MARRIAGE

Rose

Rose on my pillow
on the wedding night
trips to Mexico Bahamas
friends for dinner gourmet no less
our own bottled wine
his grandchildren visit
one delicious summer
ice cream cones marshmallow roasts

A short second marriage four years
and now since the stroke
he drags his left leg
we never go for walks he cannot
speak just a word or two
before the crying sputtering starts
eats slowly fear of choking
half his throat is paralyzed
his smile crooked when I serve him
coffee in the morning
brown spills on the towel arranged around his neck

Bob sits in an easy chair
watches weather channel curtains closed
sometimes I take him for a drive
in the mountains watch a Saturday
night movie lying together
in our big bed does he remember

the long stemmed rose before
he falls asleep mouth open snoring

I tip-toe into spare bedroom sip
a glass of wine read
turn out the light

Meditation (Riffing on *Muse* by David Zieroth)

He is in the next room
He is not in the next room

He is on a cruise ship
looking through binoculars
photographs egrets and osprey
foraging in ocean inlets
studies amethysts emeralds
buys a strand of diamonds
to wrap around my throat

He is undressing
come to bed
He has the face of confusion
furrows in his brow
stubble more than a day's worth on his chin
stumbles and falls into the armchair
His hands shake step unsure on
our broadloom rug
I take his arm on the pathway
watch a bald eagle alight on a snag
branch breaks bird falls to the ground
recovers flies away
My husband grabs the garage door opener
tries to unlock the car
with this gadget he no longer understands
and neither does my heart

A Real Gentleman

Bob my husband is a gentleman from Virginia
on our first date and for nights after that
he brought me a single rose
May I kiss upon you he'd say
extend his hand the flower
slide his arm around my waist

Bob my husband is a gentleman from Virginia
after the first stroke he could hardly talk dragged one foot
after the second stroke he had foecal accidents
after the third I was told not to worry about his crying

Bob my husband is a gentleman from Virginia
we moved to the States his family
could help take care of him
I got a job in New York

Bob my husband is a gentleman from Virginia
who I found out hadn't paid his taxes
so five years ago he fled to Canada
from Internal Revenue

Bob my husband is a gentleman from Virginia
who now lives in a nursing home
in Alberta in the home
he has a girlfriend Adele

a born again Christian
She calls him *Honey*
slaps her hand over her mouth *woops*
when I get up to leave he reaches
for the walker *It's okay*
You don't have to see me to the door.
You've got company
But there's nothing like a wife
says Adele at that last visit

WIDOW

Enchanted Evening

Saturday night at Singles Club
we sit at dinner tables
white cloth a candle
each of us buys our own
glass of wine

Men boast about their fishing trips kayaks vintage cars
a chorus of frogs singing
women freshen up lipstick hide a bra strap suck tic tacs
skittish mares waiting to be mounted

Small talk over dessert
How long have you been divorced?
Seven years. You?
Widowed
disc jockey tests the sound system
over ebullient chatter

One or two women
go to Ladies' Room floss
men already know who
they will choose for the
first dance

Half way through the evening
Ladies' Choice
in case too many sit alone
shoes off under table

By ten thirty lucky ones
are coupled his hand on
the small of her back
he asks the important question
Can I take you home?
they cut across
the uncertain
dance floor dodging sweating swaying bodies

The rest of us find our own way home
in car
taxi
sky train
and nurse a scotch
before bed

Woman of Samaria

who is this man
drinks from my jar
in heat of the noonday sun
calls me sister takes my heart
hardened passed from man to man
five or twenty I never can keep count
cups the brittle beating thing
in slender fingers white as feathers
warm as wings 'til it cracks open
like the porous rock of Moses
brimful of tears before I ask

is this the living water
he blows those shards
from the palm of his hand
small fragments like letters
of the alphabet my story
carried on wind into the heart of God

who is this man
who claims *you shall never thirst again*

Grandmother

I watch baby's head crown
emerge from cocoon
of my daughter's soft flesh
it's here I shout *it's over*
strangers gather round her open legs
purple bands of pulpy tissue exposed
ribbons of blood stitch her up
too much blood too late to freeze
David holds the baby to Celeste's face
tries to distract her
from the sting of needles
probe of unfamiliar fingers
she barely smiles turns away into
contours of comfortless white pillow
stifles a moan

Question

My granddaughter plays with her doll's house
tiny stove bed kitchen table and chairs
miniature mother baby and grandfather
This is God she says
holds up the old man
I shake my head *no*
God is spirit like the wind
Yahweh feel breath on your lips

But what does God look like? Ava asks
God is like the ocean and we the fish
water around us within us
gushing through our gills
aflame with the rush of tides

What is his name?
There are 99 names for God
But who is he?
The Mysterium Tremendum

Not true This is God
She clutches the white-haired bearded doll

FINAL CURTAIN

Gethsemane

Teenage boy in a hospital bed
cancer of the leg he waits for amputation
his hour in Gethsemane

Young man checks controls
first bombing mission over Iraq
waits for take-off
his hour in Gethsemane

Mother single parent
three mouths to feed waits for envelope
pink slip her hour in Gethsemane

Veteran panhandling on Hastings Street
binning tonight in the alley
his hour in Gethsemane

Syrian refugee playing in hotel room lobby
hoping for housing soon and her own bed
night terrors her hour in Gethsemane

If I had been with Jesus
the night he was betrayed
I would have held him
a motherly embrace
for a man who thinks
he is too old too brave to cry

This cup will not pass let me
stay with you until the end

His answer
Remain here and watch
with me in hospital corridor
cockpit line up at food bank
Hastings Street and hotel lobby

The Trial

1. Barabbas

No wonder we chose Barabbas
What could Jesus offer
the bandit couldn't top
poverty broken spirit contrite heart?
hardly subjects for dead time
between evening news and sports
No one wants to hunger and thirst after justice
become a peace maker
or suffer persecution
even if it is for righteousness' sake

Barabbas comes down to our level
knows how to strike a deal
reduce taxable income
which future's stock to buy
how to jump bail skip alimony payments

I wonder how Jesus felt
sitting in the jail house
hearing the crowd call out
Barrabas free Barrabas

He brought it on himself
was really serious
about giving a beggar

a coat and cloak also
building low-income housing
sponsoring refugees from Syria
setting up a woman's shelter
in our neighbourhood

We donate to charity
give blood belong to Rotary
How far are you supposed to go?
In the end Barrabas was the safest bet
He doesn't want to change the world
Neither do we

2. Herod

Herod looked forward to the trial
always wanted to meet Jesus
hoped for some signs or wonders
to talk about at the next cocktail party

The prisoner remained silent
if he had cooperated
Herod would have spared the man
offered him a seat in the next election
since he was interested in social justice
or a post at the new university
in Jerusalem something in philosophy
or world religions

There was nothing left to do
but send him back to Pilate
who admitted *He hasn't broken
any laws in my book*
The prisoner had no political savvy
didn't even try to negotiate
make a trade-off compromise a little

Herod said *He was a big
disappointment* the best thing
about the day was that he and Pilate became friends
after that terrible fall-out
over the weapons treaty and sale of arms.

At My Dying

Robin alights on broken branch
split by frost warbles *tut-tut-tut*
to distant Spring Blackbird
wing tip red perched on dry reed
sings in farmer's field *o-ka-lay*
awaits summer fires

Orange oriole brighter
than yellow elm pipes her discontent
hew-li at falling leaves

Blizzard obliterates tracks in snow
and owl booms *who-hoo-hoo*
at frozen corpse *Tut-tut–tut*
o- ka–lay hew-li
who-hoo–hoo silence angel choirs
sing dirges at my dying
with your sweet pandemonium

Make My Coffin Wide

when I die make my coffin
wide so I can spread my legs
that's how I spent most of my life

spread your legs tuck in your butt
point your toes flex and point
bend your knees that's it ladies one, two three

spread your legs stretch and bend
clean the toilet hang up the clothes
sew and mend unwind the hose
that Harry forgot to put away last summer

when you're tired spread your legs
in a hot tub filled with bubbles
that is   after you've scrubbed it
'cause nobody else will

spread your legs c'mon Honey open wide
sorry about last night what's the matter forget the fight

spread your legs I can see his head
breathe deeply just like I said
don't push   that's it   relax
good girl

spread your legs a little bit more
this may hurt a tiny sore

just like a bee sting
don't move your legs relax

spread your legs first one then the other
it's easier that way we don't want you to fall between
the bed and the stretcher
we'll support your shoulder
just slide over that's it good girl

when I die make my coffin wide
so I can stretch out on either side
point my toes tuck in my pelvis
breathe deeply count to four
relax and spread my legs

Last Act

My son says
move now before you break a hip, a collar bone before
pneumonia or the final flu
close to family Sunday dinners grandchildren check in
to see if you`re still moving still alive

Goodbye to my home view of harbour
seagulls screeching flapping
the Quay its revolving red Q
restaurants at waterside
tandoori chicken sushi beaver tails
breakfast on my balcony where pigeons play
May flowers spring up in clay pots

No to Care Centre tasteless lasagna
pungent meat loaf oversweet cupcakes
after country-western songs about love gone wrong
no to Depends Ensure
before I forget my name and yours
before I`ll submit to staff in Special Care Unit

Nothing special there
but locked doors hair dresser
who perms straight hair to sausage curls nurse
who washes roughly under arm
scratches nipples scrapes cunt
bingo bridge recreation therapist
today we'll spatter paint Tomorrow...

Flee to Stanley Park dodge police cars
steal Missing Person posters burn picture in a bonfire lit
by homeless man bathe naked in English Bay at midnight
sleep under an arching Arbutus
pick daisies poke flowers behind my ears
fall asleep in The Fifth Avenue Cinema
dream I crush a cigarette under my stiletto
become Humphrey Bogart's most unusual suspect
take a Marilyn Munroe pose over a subway grating
show off my stork-like legs, varicose veins
Attend a Baptist church con the choir into singing
Lulu's back in town.

Afterword

Sit quietly, and listen for a voice that will say, Be more silent.
—Rumi

I was inspired to write many of these poems when I experienced forty days of silence at Loyola House in Guelph, Ontario. In the gracious company of Jesuits, I made the spiritual exercises of Saint Ignatius. Each day is spent reflecting on an episode in the life of Jesus. But one doesn't just remember the events. One becomes a character in the scene. For instance, when I reflected on the Nativity, I imagined myself as the innkeeper's wife who helped Mary through her labour. Acting as a midwife, I was the first person to hold Jesus in my arms. In this way the retreatant interacts with Jesus and those whom he loved: his mother Mary, the leper, the woman of Samaria and others. One can feel the sand between one's toes, smell the Sea of Galilee, taste the fish, and talk to Mary Magdalene. Over the course of the day personal memories surface and the stories and incidents co-mingle. Sometimes I was overcome with sadness and at other times I felt great peace.

This book is a diary, a record of my relationships: with family, with the world, and most significantly with the Divine. Long ago, the Hebrew people believed they carried Yahweh in the Ark of the Covenant. As they wandered through the desert God accompanied them. My poems are my Ark, my way of holding the presence or the absence of the Holy.

Acknowledgements

I began writing this collection when I took an evening class with Doug Barbour at the University of Alberta and continued working on it when I attended a silent retreat at Loyola House in Guelph. I stuffed the manuscript in a drawer and forgot about it until I decided to join a poetry workshop through the Writers Studio at Simon Fraser University. My gratitude goes out to Evelyn Lau for her insistence that this book see the light of day, and for her enduring friendship. Many thanks to Fiona Tinwei Lam for her kindness and for teaching me new forms that gave my poems life and vitality. To Betsy Warland, the founder and first director of the Writer's Studio, I give thanks for her generosity, encouragement, and continuous faith in me. And to Wayde Compton who accepted me into graduate workshops at the Writer's Studio and has continued to be a support. I will always be thankful for all my enthusiastic colleagues at the Writer's Studio who are too many to mention by name.

I was diagnosed with Stage Four pancreatic cancer after this book was accepted for publication. My friends and cohorts at the Writer's Studio rallied to get this manuscript published earlier, and for that I am profoundly grateful. My thanks and gratitude also go out to Luciana Ricciutelli, Editor-in-Chief at Inanna Publications, for working so hard to move the publication date forward. I am so pleased and happy!

To my children, Rhiannon and Alexander, who have supported me throughout my artistic journey, and to their spouses Jason and Delyana, and my grandchildren Ava, Luke, Vivian, Dalia, and Doroteya, who have provided loving encouragement as well as inspiration for many of these poems. Much love to you all!

Photo: Ayelet Tsabari

Cullene Bryant is a retired minister in the United Church of Canada and grandmother of five children. She worked most of her life as a teaching chaplain in hospitals in Toronto, Edmonton, New York, and the Philippines have been home for me. She studied at the Centre for Spirituality and Justice in New York and received a Doctor of Ministry from Princeton in New Jersey. She is the author of two collections of short fiction, *Llamas In The Snow* (1993) and *In the Dry Woods* (2005). The title story of the latter collection, "In The Dry Woods," was awarded the 2006 national Canadian Christian Writing Award. Her stories have aired on CBC radio and appeared in various literary journals, among them *Room of One's Own; Fiddlehead; Descant* and *The Iowa Review*. *God is a Laughing Bedouin* is her first poetry collection. She lives in North Vancouver, British Columbia.